CANDLES

CANDLES

Illuminating Ideas For Creative Candlemaking
and Enchanting Displays

Gloria Nicol

LORENZ BOOKS

First published in 1999 by Lorenz Books

© Anness Publishing Limited 1999

Lorenz Books is an imprint of
Anness Publishing Limited
Hermes House
88-89 Blackfriars Road
London SE1 8HA

Published in the USA by Lorenz Books
Anness Publishing Inc., 27 West 20th Street, New York, NY 10011;
(800) 354-9657

This edition distributed in Canada by Raincoast Books
8680 Cambie Street, Vancouver, British Columbia V6P 6M9

A CIP catalogue record for this book is available from the British Library

ISBN 0 7548 0188 8

Publisher: Joanna Lorenz
Senior Editor: Joanne Rippen
Special Photography: Debbie Patterson
Designer: Nigel Partridge
Production Controller: Karina Han
Additional projects: p34/35 & 60/61 Diana Civil, photography by Russel Sadur; p36/37 Stephanie
Donaldson, photography by Michelle Garrett; p48/49 & 58/59 Tessa Evelegh, photography by
Debbie Patterson, Styled by Tessa Evelagh; p50/51 Deena Beverley,
photgraphy by Michelle Garrett.

Printed and bound in Singapore

1 3 5 7 9 10 8 6 4 2

CONTENTS

INTRODUCTION 7

CANDLEMAKING 19

DECORATING CANDLES 41

HOLDERS AND CONTAINERS 55

INDEX 64

INTRODUCTION

EVERY ROOM IN A HOUSE OR APARTMENT CAN BENEFIT
FROM THE MAGIC THAT CANDLE FLAMES PROVIDE.
LIGHTING A CANDLE BRINGS INSTANT ATMOSPHERE TO
THE SURROUNDINGS. CHANGE THE WAY YOU USE
THEM TO CREATE DIFFERENT STYLES AND THEMES, AND
TO CREATE ELEGANT DISPLAYS THAT HIGHLIGHT
FEATURES OF A ROOM.

TOP: *Match rustic stoneware with exotic blooms for
a simple spring display.*

LEFT: *Plain, carved and twisted white and cream candles
allied to the delicate stems of snowberries make the most
imaginative candle display for a winter wedding.*

CANDLES IN THE HOME

Before gas and electricity became common sources of power available to everyone, candles were the only source of artificial light. From early times, candles and tapers were made by dipping rushes into tallow, an animal fat which produces black smoke and an appalling stench when burned. Better-quality candles were made from beeswax but only the rich and the clergy could afford them. It was not

Below: Living flames, in the fireplace and above it, impart a warm glow.

until the mid-19th century that the development of stearin as a chemical compound, originally produced from refined fat, changed the technique of candlemaking, to give the longer burning, odour-free candles that we can buy today.

Now, even though they are no longer a necessity, we still choose to use candles, not only for their decorative qualities but because of something even more special that attracts us to them. Candles have the ability to change the mood of the room, create an atmosphere, and enchant with their flickering beauty.

CANDLES FOR DECORATION

Whether lit or unlit, candles add special qualities to both formal and informal surroundings, and can fit into any room. They should not be reserved just for special occasions – there is no reason why their beauty and elegance should not be enjoyed on a daily basis.

Place them carefully in the room for a particular effect. Candles that will be lit regularly should be placed so that they make a focal point in the room, where you can make the most of the

Above: Candles bring their charm to even the most informal setting.

light they give. Make sure candles are placed out of the way of draughts as these cause candles to burn unevenly.

EATING BY CANDLELIGHT

Dining rooms and tables provide a perfect setting for candle arrangements at both formal and informal occasions.

A low central table setting of candles and fresh flowers, or holders arranged symmetrically, will not get in the way. If a centrepiece is out of the question, then individual candles can be placed beside each place setting.

ABOVE: A beautifully contrived table setting with worn terracotta pots filled with candles that complement the earthenware and antique pine table.

BELOW: Simple metal holders, and natural-coloured candles and soaps, suit this country-style bathroom.

CANDLES IN THE KITCHEN

A lot of time is spent in the kitchen, and candles can be used to great effect there, though you need to be careful where they are placed.

In a busy kitchen, a wire fruit bowl, with candleholders incorporated into its design, will make a useful centrepiece, with the varieties and colours of the replenished fruits providing an ever-changing effect. This type of container provides a good, steady base.

A simple cast-iron chandelier over the table, where people will be seated for meals makes a good focal point, especially when all the candles are lit. Be careful of dripping wax.

BATHROOMS

The best bathrooms provide a haven of peace and privacy. Candles help to create a relaxed atmosphere.

Lanterns and chandeliers are excellent in bathrooms because they do not encroach on valuable surface areas, and they look most exotic. A bracket shelf in a corner, or wall sconces, are other places where candles can be sited.

Candles can be bought moulded in the shape of Marseille soaps and placed beside the real thing for an original, harmonious touch.

BELOW: A bathroom benefits from the magic of candlelight that creates a warm and sensuous atmosphere. Blue candles tone in with the decor.

CANDLE THEMES

The creative potential for displaying candles in the home often goes unrealized. Candles and candle holders come in so many shapes and sizes that they are an ideal way of enhancing a decorating theme and they can be chosen to suit any particular style, whether it be classical, simple, rustic or ethnic.

Many items from the house, or even the garden, can be turned into innovative candle holders, extending the options for decorating with candles.

LEFT: *Turned wooden candlesticks, with painted and varnished finishes, fit perfectly into a country kitchen.*

ABOVE: *Decorative tulip candlesticks are part of this floral design which displays blooms and candles together.*

SIMPLE PURITY

For a look imbued with simple purity, choose an all-white or cream colour theme. This approach fits into any setting and has universal freshness. Creamware candlesticks, available in age-old designs, with pale beeswax candles provide the starting point and a group of these displayed on linen- or lace-covered tables, will instantly produce a magical effect. White flowers, with a trace of green or the faintest pink blush, can be added to include a suggestion of colour.

GOTHIC SPLENDOUR

Conjuring up turreted castles and medieval splendour, Gothic style is bold and theatrical. Candles, chandeliers and floor-standing candelabra were

ABOVE: An elegant display of candles in a cream ceramic candle holder, with a few blooms of white ranunculus.

then use heraldic motifs and ecclesiastical designs to embellish your displays of candles.

Simple but bold accessories made from brass, bronze, iron and wood, go very well with this look, as do turned wooden bowls and heavy glass goblets. Church and beeswax candles are an obvious choice to include in a Gothic display, but look out as well for other, more ornate candles which have the right feel and will add a finishing touch to your creation.

ABOVE: The simple, cream candles of this display contrast beautifully with the bright-red parrot tulips.

an important part of this look in the 16th century, so using them to create a period illusion works perfectly. Scale everything down to manageable proportions that suit your own home, and

FLORAL ARRANGEMENTS

Candles can be included in flower arrangements to add another dimension to the design, incorporating their

own ornamental and decorative qualities among the plant materials. When the candles are lit, they draw attention to individual flowers and leaves. You might want to use candles in an arrangement for a particularly special occasion, to add an extra element to a floral centrepiece for an evening dinner table or, as part of a larger scheme, to decorate a mantelpiece.

Flowers will conjure a seasonal look beautifully, whether you use evergreens at Christmas, or primroses in spring.

LEFT: Brass candle holders with attractive openwork decoration are most appropriate for Gothic style. They need substantial pillar candles to balance their proportions. A simple brass candlestick with a fleur-de-lys stem completes the picture.

ABOVE: Ivy, replete with its autumn berries, makes a lovely dark-green background to the three church candles. Although simple, this arrangement conveys a classical perfection.

CELESTIAL

Stars, suns and moons are popular decorative motifs which always fascinate and attract. Use candles to embellish a celestial theme with gold as the predominant colour and the heavenly symbols will add their own impact.

Candlelight looks wonderful when reflected and radiating from gold surfaces; it extends the light and gives it a shimmering warmth all around. Brass lanterns, gilded wood and metal candlesticks are all easy to find. Group them closely and complete the arrangement by adding gilded angels and cherubs to the display.

COUNTRY STYLE

Candles fit perfectly into a simple country setting, evoking the days when candles were the only light source after sunset. Candlemaking used to be one of the apiarist's essential skills, using the beeswax that remains after honey

BELOW: Stars, moons, pomegranates and a cherub make a heavenly scene. Beeswax candles add their golden colouring to the picture.

is removed from a comb. Beeswax in natural shades has been used for centuries to make fragrant and slow-burning candles. Candles in the shape of old-fashioned coiled beehives capture a rustic style instantly. Old, turned wooden and painted candlesticks help to add to the country feel.

PROVENÇAL STYLE

Provence, in southern France, is an area renowned for its lavender. To bring some of the area's style and warmth into your home use dried lavender to make pretty collars to decorate the base of your candles and lend its unmistakable fragrance to the room.

ABOVE: A verdigris-coloured finish on metal candlesticks gives them an antique look and a country feel.

OPPOSITE: Scented candles surrounded by lavender collars are a perfect reminder of holidays in Provence.

Tie the flowers together in small bunches and secure with florist's wire. Cut the stems to the same length. Bend some wire into a ring that fits comfortably around the base of the candle. Wind several thicknesses of wire around the ring, then lay the bunches one by one around it, pointing in the same direction. Secure them with wire and finish with a ribbon.

SEASONAL CANDLES

In the same way that flora and fauna change in an annual cycle, with the colours of flowers and plants indicating the time of year, candles can be used as part of sumptuous displays to celebrate the passing of the seasons. You can buy moulded candles in the shapes of flowers and leaves which conjure up the atmosphere of the

BELOW: The yellow flame of the candles burning in mossy pots complements the delicate colour of the primroses. Spring bulbs growing in weathered terracotta pots complete the picture.

ABOVE: Egg-shaped candles make a lovely spring or Easter arrangement.

season, and there are many simple ideas for decorative touches which can reflect the time of year.

SPRING

The first flowers of spring, such as snowdrops, narcissi and primroses, provide a pastel palette of colours that combine beautifully with candles. There is always a feeling of optimism and excitement as the garden comes to life and begins again its yearly cycle. In spring, the evenings still draw in early enough to benefit from the magic of candlelight. Mossy pots make pretty containers for candles and are easy to make. If you can find them, use old, weathered terracotta plant pots to hold the candles.

SUMMER

During the long days of summer, the garden and outdoor living dominate the lifestyles of many. Fine weather and warm sunny days mean more time can be spent outside; and candlelight and garden flares can be used to decorate the garden. Candles and lanterns can be used to illuminate tables for alfresco

BELOW: Novelty candles can be found shaped like many flowers in the garden in the summer. You could add fragrant oils to the wick to enhance the pleasure of this summer arrangement.

ABOVE: An artless, imaginative display that is carefully placed but looks natural, and echoes the fruits of autumn. The floral motif on the candlesticks provides a finishing touch.

dining, as the sun sets. Windows and doors leading to the garden are likely to be kept open. Use brightly coloured candles that echo the colours of flowers growing outside to bring the garden inside, and fill baskets of flowers mingled with candles in an arrangement. Make sure candles are placed high enough above the flowers, so that when they are lit they don't damage the blooms. Replace them as soon as they burn too low.

AUTUMN

In the "season of mists and mellow fruitfulness", the countryside changes to subtle shades of russet, bronze, brown and gold. Although the year starts to wind down, it is a time of great abundance with a rich harvest of fruits and berries. Use these for your decorative ideas.

Berried foliage and gently dying leaves are perfect partners for candlelight and provide opportunities for decorating the house. Candles are available to complement all of these shades and lend a touch of warmth during the cold months ahead. Wrap autumn leaves around the base of some candles: the larger the leaves the bigger the candle you will need. You can also find wonderful candles in shapes of autumn fruits and leaves.

WINTER

During the cold months of winter, the garden lies dormant and the daylight hours are at their shortest. Now, candles come into their own to lift the spirits. As well as branches of colourful berries that can be used in winter candle displays, other elements can be drawn from the season to create a particular look. Shop-bought candles made to look like bare twigs match the bareness of the trees outside and help to create a winter look. But with a little imagination many other ideas can be realized.

BELOW: In winter, choose frosted glass candlesticks and night-light holders to echo the winter snow and frost outside. Glass tumblers work just as well if they are lit by night-lights.

SPECIAL OCCASIONS BY CANDLELIGHT

ABOVE: Make an Advent wreath to mark off the four weeks to Christmas.

BELOW: A traditional Christmas look with contemporary freshness.

Throughout the year our lives are plotted around significant occasions marked on the calendar. Candlelight adds a touch of magic to any special day and can help to turn it into a real celebration.

WEDDING

The romance of candlelight and weddings go hand in hand, especially if you use candles to decorate the tables for a reception or evening party. Popular floral colours include classic white and creams with lilies and stephanotis, but try using deep pastel-coloured candles

ABOVE: Thick pillar candles, supported on simple squares of marble, are ideal for a wedding party.

and bright cottage garden flowers or even rich burgundy and russet shades for an autumn wedding.

CHRISTMAS

Christmas is the perfect time to deck your home with an abundance of winter evergreens and brightly coloured decorations. At Christmas it is impossible to have too many candles. Group them together for maximum effect,

ABOVE: A birthday cake topped with traditional twisted candles, and surrounded by other decorations.

you burn, and set up arrangements on every available surface. Use frosted glass, silver trays, shiny balls and anything else that will catch the light and reflect it into the room. Use candles in deep reds and greens as well as traditional cream-coloured church candles.

HALLOWE'EN

Candlelight forms an intrinsic part of the atmosphere on Hallowe'en: hollowed pumpkins are carved by children to make lanterns with simple ghoulish faces that the candlelight will glow through. Pumpkin carving can be

BELOW: Hollowed-out pumpkins make the most effective Hallowe'en lanterns.

much more decorative however, and you can create unusual designs of swirling filigree lines, stars and leaf shapes which look spectacular. Use a small sharp knife or a lino or wood-cutting tool to cut the designs. Remember to incorporate holes so that the candle will have enough air.

BIRTHDAY

Blowing out the candles on a birthday cake and making a wish, is part of traditional birthday celebrations. The little candles are lit, blown out and removed from the cake in moments, however. So to prolong the festivities, surround the cake with novelty candles that will burn for much longer.

and display them in candleholders in festive colours and shapes. The countdown to Christmas is a large part of the excitement and fun of the impending celebrations, especially for children, and it is a wonderful idea to make an Advent ring. Make a decorative wreath of fresh foliage and fruits that holds four candles within its circle. One candle is lit to mark each of the four weeks before Christmas.

For the Christmas celebrations themselves, make sure you have a large stock of candles to replace the ones

CANDLEMAKING

THE ART OF CANDLEMAKING HAS COME A LONG WAY FROM THE DAYS WHEN CANDLES WERE THE ONLY MEANS OF LIGHTING A HOME AFTER SUNSET. IF YOU MAKE YOUR OWN, YOU CAN USE YOUR SKILLS TO CREATE ALL KINDS OF SHAPES, SIZES AND DESIGNS. USE THE BASIC SKILLS IN THE FOLLOWING PAGES TO START WITH, AND THEN LET YOUR IMAGINATION TAKE FLIGHT.

TOP: *An old silver candelabra is embellished with twining ivy, and fresh flowers.*

LEFT: *Wax can be carved, moulded, rolled, or dipped to make an endless variety of brilliantly coloured candles.*

MATERIALS

For centuries, candles were simply made from wax and wicks. Nowadays, the candlemaker can make candles in all shapes and sizes, and can add dyes and perfumes to increase the pleasure of making and burning candles in the home.

Wax is the primary ingredient for candlemaking. To measure how much you need, fill the candle mould with water. For every 100 ml (3½ fl oz) of water you will need 90 g (3½ oz) of cold wax.

PARAFFIN WAX
This is the basic wax used for candlemaking. It is generally sold in bead or pellet form and melts at a temperature between 40–71°C (104–160°F).

BEESWAX
This natural product can be bought in shades of brown or in bleached white. It is quite expensive, but worth buying for the wonderful perfume it gives off. Generally, it is used in combination with other waxes to increase the burning time of the candle. It can also be bought in sheets for making simple rolled candles.

If more than 10 per cent of beeswax is used for making a moulded candle, you need to apply a releasing agent to the mould as the wax is sticky.

DIP AND CARVE WAX
This type of wax is available in large chunks. It is a blend of waxes specially formulated so that it can be carved without splitting. It is slightly more malleable than ordinary wax and can be used for moulds as well as dipping.

STEARIN
This is added to paraffin wax so that candles are easier to release from their moulds. It also helps to stop candles from dripping. You need to add one

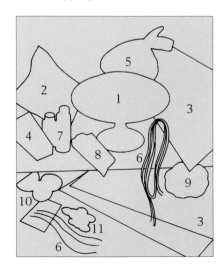

part stearin for every 10 parts wax. If you are using dye, add it to the stearin before you add the wax. Paraffin wax with stearin already added is available.

WAX DYE
Wax can be dyed in a vast spectrum of colours using wax dyes in disc or powder form. The dye needs to be quite strong to be effective.

WAX GLUE
This is a soft, sticky wax that is available in solid form. Use it to glue pieces of wax together and also to stick decorations to a candle.

CANDLE PERFUME
You only need a few drops of perfume. Add it when the wax has melted.

LEFT (KEY):1. Paraffin wax, 2. Beeswax, 3. Beeswax sheets, 4. Dip and carve wax, 5. Stearin, 6. Primed (right) and unprimed (left) wicks, 7. Candle scent, 8. Wax glue, 9. Mould seal, 10. Dye, 11. Wick sustainers (wick supports).

MOULD SEAL

This sticky, putty-like substance makes moulds watertight, and is also used to secure the wick in a mould. Remove any seal from the wick as even a small amount will stop it burning.

WICKS

Choosing the right wick for the right candle is essential. Wicks are usually made from braided cotton, and are sold according to the diameter of the candle you are making; sizes range from 1–10cm (½–4in), in 1cm (½in) gradations. You therefore need a 2.5cm (1in) wick for a candle 2.5cm (1in) in diameter, and so on. You can also buy special wicks for containers, available in small, medium and large sizes from 5–15cm (2–6in). Metal-core wicks are specifically designed for longer burning candles and should be used in container candles. Similarly, floating candles require a special floating-candle wick. Wicks need to be primed before use. Soak in paraffin wax for five minutes and leave to dry.

WICK SUSTAINERS (WICK SUPPORTS)

These are used to anchor the wick in container candles. Push the wick into the sustainer (support) and pinch the metal together so that it sits flat on the base of the container.

EQUIPMENT

Candlemaking does not require a vast amount of specialist equipment – a good many items can be found in any kitchen. You will, however, need a dipping can – if you want to make candles the old-fashioned way – a wax thermometer, wicking needles and various moulds.

Look out for unusual items to use as moulds or candle holders, and start to build up a collection of candlemaking equipment.

DOUBLE BOILER

Ideally, this should be made of stainless steel or aluminium, and once you have used it for candlemaking it shouldn't be used for cooking. You can improvise by placing one saucepan over another, or putting a bowl to rest on a saucepan, but take special care as the wax may melt at an uneven pace.

Boil the water in the bottom of the pan and melt the wax in the top part. Make sure the water in the bottom pan does not boil dry, and keep it topped up as necessary. To clean the double boiler after use, wipe around the inside with kitchen paper.

DIPPING CAN

A tall, cylindrical container available from good craft shops and candlemakers' suppliers, it is used to hold liquid wax. The container may take more wax than you think it needs, so make sure you have some spare to add. Stand the container in a pan of simmering water, with the water level as high as possible to keep the wax liquid.

WAX THERMOMETER

When you are making candles the wax must be heated to certain temperatures. You may be able to use a cooking or candy thermometer, so long as its gauge covers the same scale as a special wax thermometer – 38–108°C

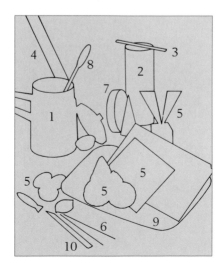

(100–226°F). Never leave melting wax unattended – it can catch alight and is as volatile as hot oil.

GREASEPROOF (WAXED) PAPER

If you have any wax left over when you have finished making your candles, line an old baking pan with greaseproof (waxed) paper and pour the wax into it. Leave it to set and you can then remelt it and use it again.

MOULDS

Glass moulds can be used almost indefinitely, so long as you manage not to break them. Plastic and rubber moulds have a more limited life. Plastic moulds are less expensive than glass, and rubber ones more ornate. You can also buy

LEFT (KEY): 1. Double boiler, 2. Dipping can, 3. Wax thermometer, 4. Greaseproof (waxed) paper, 5. A selection of moulds, and small tins that act as moulds, 6. Wicking needles, 7. Cake ring, 8. Spoon or stirrer, 9. Baking pan, 10. Scalpel or craft knife.

spherical and egg-shaped moulds that come apart in the middle. Moulds are available in an infinite variety of shapes.

WICKING NEEDLES

These are made of steel and come in various sizes between 10–25cm (4–10in) long. They are used for inserting wicks and securing the wick at the base of the mould.

CAKE RING

This is not an essential item. However, it is an excellent example of equipment that you may already have in the kitchen which can be adapted to make a mould.

SPOON OR STIRRER

If you do not have an old spoon, you can use a wooden stick. You do not have to stir wax while it is melting, but you do need to stir when you add dye.

OLD BAKING PAN

This, or something similar, is useful as a water bath for cooling small floating candles while they set.

SCALPEL OR CRAFT KNIFE

A scalpel or craft knife is useful for cutting wicks to length, trimming candles, cutting beeswax sheets and cutting out a template or stencil.

DIPPING CANDLES

Dipped candles are easy to make and have an elegance all of their own. They can be coloured by making them from dyed wax or you can add a coloured outer coating to white candles. Take care to heat the wax to the correct temperature — this takes practice.

YOU WILL NEED
- *large saucepan*
- *metal dipping can*
- *paraffin wax*
- *spoon or stick for stirring*
- *wax thermometer*
- *wax dye*
- *lengths of primed wick 60cm (24in) for each pair of 25cm (10in) candles*
- *sharp knife*

1 Fill the saucepan with water. Put the dipping can in the saucepan and pour in the paraffin wax. Heat the water to slowly melt the wax, stirring occasionally. Test the temperature of the liquid wax with the wax thermometer. When it has reached 71°C (160°F), turn down the heat.

2 To colour the wax, add pieces of solid dye, stirring as you do so to mix the two together. Do not add too much. If you want to strengthen the colour after you have made one pair of candles, you can always add more dye to the remaining melted wax.

3 Check that the temperature of the wax is 71°C (160°F). Hold a length of wick in the middle, and dip the two ends into the wax so that about 5cm (2in) on either side of your fingers remains uncovered. Keep the wicks in the wax for about 3 seconds.

HINTS AND TIPS

Making candles by dipping is the oldest of all methods and extends back to Medieval times. Dipped candles are easy to make and have a unique tapered shape unmatched by any factory-made candle. Candles are made a pair at a time by repeatedly dipping a double loop of wick into molten wax. You can make solid coloured candles with a coloured wax, or colour them by overdipping white candles in coloured wax. Holding the wick so that the pairs of candles are kept apart as they dry can take a bit of practice. They seem to have an almost magnetic attraction to each other as you lift the tapers out of the wax. Hang pairs up, held apart over two nails, or alternatively over a slat of wood, to cool for at least 1 hour before lighting them.

4 Remove the wicks and leave them to cool for about 3 minutes, hanging on a peg or pair of nails so they dry without touching. Repeat the dipping and drying 15–30 times until the candles are the right thickness.

5 For a smooth surface, increase the heat of the wax to 82°C (180°F) for the final dipping. When the candles have cooled, trim the base flat with a sharp knife.

RIGHT: Brightly coloured dipped tapers look decorative even when they are not lit. As a dipping can needs a lot of wax to fill it, it is a good idea to make several pairs at a time.

MOULDING CANDLES

The candlemaker can achieve the most extraordinary effects using simple moulds. Start with moulds based on geometric shapes and then let your fancy take you where you wish. Moulds are relatively inexpensive and can be used over and over again.

YOU WILL NEED
- *primed wick*
- *mould*
- *wicking needle*
- *mould seal*
- *stearin (10% of quantity of wax)*
- *double boiler*
- *wax dye*
- *spoon or stick for stirring*
- *paraffin wax*
- *wax thermometer*
- *bowl/container as deep as the mould*
- *weight*
- *needle*
- *scissors*

WAX REQUIRED

To calculate the amount of wax you will need for a mould, fill the mould with water and measure it – for every 100ml (3½fl oz) of water you will need 90g (3oz) of cold wax.

Most moulded candles start with a primed wick of a grade corresponding to the candle size. You will need a length of wick about 5cm (2in) longer than the candle.

MOULD SEAL

Always use plenty of mould seal to make the mould watertight. Some moulds have a base platform or flat end to help keep them upright and steady, while others need to be given some support. Rubber and glass moulds with a lipped edge can be suspended through a cardboard collar to hold them vertical.

COOLING

Where possible, use a water bath to help to shorten the cooling time. Candles can be left to cool at room temperature, but water cooling improves their appearance.

Use a container with a level base, roomy enough to fill with water to within 1cm (½in) of the top of the inverted mould. Always fill the container with water to the correct height before putting in the mould.

1 Thread a primed wick through the hole in the base of the mould. Tie the wick around the centre of the wicking needle to hold it firmly at the top of the mould. Then pull the other (burning) end of the wick so that it is taut and press a generous amount of mould seal around it. Check that the mould is watertight.

►

RIGHT: Jewel-coloured star candles and straight-sided pillars are easy to make, and look good in a group. The wax has been dyed to give a vibrant range of colours in burnt orange, deep purple and crimson, which look stunning together. Even when candles have a solid steady base, it is best to place them on dishes, plates or tiles.

2 Melt the stearin in the double boiler and add the dye, breaking it into pieces. Stir them in until they are completely melted.

3 Add the paraffin wax to the double boiler and melt it. Test the temperature with the thermometer. When the melted wax reaches 93°C (200°F), pour it into the centre of the mould, taking care not to let the wax splash on to the sides. Leave a gap of about 1cm (½in) at the top of the mould. Leave the wax to settle for a couple of minutes and then tap the side of the mould to get rid of any air bubbles.

4 Fill a container with water, full enough so that when you place the mould in it the water will come to within 1cm (½in) of the top. Do not let any water splash on to the wax. Put a weight on top of the mould to prevent it from floating. Leave it to cool for one hour.

HINTS AND TIPS
Moulds come in all shapes and sizes, from simple geometric forms, such as pyramid, pillar and cube shapes, to the more ornate shapes of fruits, vegetables and flowers. They are made of plastic, glass, metal and rubber. They are relatively inexpensive to buy, and can be used repeatedly. With most rigid moulds, around 10 per cent stearin should be added to the wax to increase the amount of shrinkage – this will help the candle to slip easily out of the mould. As beeswax is particularly sticky, a release agent should be used on the inside of rigid moulds if the wax used includes more than 10 per cent beeswax.

5 As the wax dries, a slight dip will form around the wick. Take the mould out of the water bath and prick the candle all over this dipped area. Carefully top up the candle with more wax, melted to 93°C (200°F). You need to fill the area around the wick without allowing any wax to spill down the edges of the candle.

6 Let the wax cool in the water bath until completely set and then take it out. When the mould seal is removed, the candle will slide out of the mould. Trim the wick with scissors and then stand the candle in a warm saucepan so that the base of the candle is smooth and level.

RIGHT: Moulded, twisted and embossed candles in a variety of shapes and colours. Many candles can be scented with added oils to add a delightful fragrance to the whole house.

ROLLED CANDLES

Rolled candles made from honeycomb sheets of beeswax are among the simplest and most delightful to make. Beeswax has a delicious natural smell and the attractive embossed surface adds great charm to the finished candles.

YOU WILL NEED
- *sheet of beeswax*
- *hairdryer*
- *scalpel or craft knife*
- *metal ruler*
- *wick*
- *scissors*

1 To make a tapered candle, use a rectangular sheet of beeswax. The short side of the sheet determines the height of the candle. Warm your sheet gently with a hairdryer to make it easier to work with. Cut a tiny piece of wax from a corner. Starting diagonally opposite the cut corner, cut a narrow triangular segment from the longest side.

2 Cut a wick extending about 2cm (¾in) above the height of the candle. Press the wick gently into the edge of this longer short side. Roll up the wax, checking that the wick is held closely from the first turn.

3 When you have rolled the candle, press the edge into the candle. Trim the wick, then wrap the piece of wax around to prime it for lighting.

HINTS AND TIPS
Beeswax sheets can be bought pre-formed and ready for use and need only to be warm and pliable before you begin. They are easy to work with. Paraffin wax sheets can be used in the same way, but because they tend to be brittle and rather more difficult to work with, they will require extra care to keep them warm and pliable. There is no need to prime the wick before you start to make a candle, but the burning end of the wick will need to be primed before it is set alight. To do this simply pull a small corner piece of wax from the edge of the sheet and press it around the end of the wick.

RIGHT: Rolled candles made from white beeswax sheets give a particularly stylish look. Straight-sided candles and spiralling tapers are easy to make, but a beehive is slightly more fiddly. First roll a straight pillar around the wick for the centre of the candle, then build up the shape around it, adding bands that gradually decrease in height.

CANDY TWIST CANDLES

Classic twisted spiral candles can easily be made by the home candlemaker. With just a little care, the simple dipped candle can be transformed into a symphony of rhythm and form. Short, spiral candles add a decorative quality to metal chandeliers, or character to a table setting.

YOU WILL NEED
- *newly dipped warm candle*
  (see Dipping Candles)
- *rolling pin*

1 Flatten the candle with the rolling pin on a clean, smooth surface until it is about 5mm (¼in) thick. Try not to flatten the base of the candle as it needs to fit into a holder, although if you do, it is easy to mould it back.

HINTS AND TIPS
Start with warm, hand-dipped candles. They are easy to shape so long as the candles are kept warm and malleable. For coloured spirals, overdip the tapers in vibrantly coloured wax before you twist them.

PRACTICE MAKES PERFECT
Though your first efforts may not look faultless, the candles will burn perfectly well. Some people find that it is easier to twist upside down, with the wick furthest away from the maker. Twisted candles should never drip – this only happens when the candle is in a draught or if the ingredients have been wrongly proportioned.

2 Hold the candle near the wick between the thumb and forefinger of one hand and near the base with your other hand. Keeping one hand steady, gently twist the candle with the other. You need to work quite quickly while the wax is warm enough to respond but do not be too vigorous.

3 When the candle has twists all along its length, check that the base will fit into a candleholder. If necessary, shape it with your fingers so that it is round again. Then leave the finished candle to cool for at least 1 hour before burning.

OPPOSITE: Dipped candles dipped in yellow ochre, jade green, crimson and ultramarine take on a new appearance when shaped into elegant spirals. Hand-twisting candles adds a certain style and character which will fit comfortably in either a classical or contemporary setting.

EMBOSSED CANDLES

*Corrugated cardboard can be turned into an unusual candle mould: you can experiment with a
variety of different-sized ridges and textures to complete a decorative array of candles. Natural-
coloured wax gives these textured candles a contemporary and stylish look.*

You will need
- *corrugated cardboard*
- *craft knife*
- *metal ruler*
- *plant spray*
- *strong tape*
- *plastic container lid*
- *bradawl*
- *primed wick*
- *mould seal*
- *wicking needle*
- *stearin (10% of quantity of wax)*
- *double boiler*
- *wax dye*
- *kitchen knife*
- *wooden spoon*
- *paraffin wax*
- *wax thermometer*
- *ladle*
- *scissors*

HINTS AND TIPS
Spraying the card wet with water or
silicone oil spray before you pour in
the wax helps to prevent the wax
from sticking to the cardboard.

1 Cut a rectangle of corrugated
cardboard the desired size of the
candle. Spray the cardboard
thoroughly with water, then roll it
into a cylinder.

2 Join and cover the sides of the
cylinder with strong tape. Pierce the
middle of a plastic container lid with
a bradawl and thread a primed wick
through the hole.

3 Stand the cardboard roll centrally
over the lid. Seal all around the base
of the roll with mould seal.

4 Wind the other end of the wick
around a wicking needle and rest it
across the top of the cardboard. Seal
the hole under the base of the plastic
lid with mould seal.

5 Melt the stearin in a double boiler.
Cut off the quantity of wax dye
required and add it to the stearin.
Stir until melted. Add the wax to the
mixture and heat until it reaches
82°C (180°F).

CARDBOARD MOULDS
With cardboard moulds the wax
should be a cooler temperature than
normal. Any mottled effect the cooler
wax gives works well with this style.

6 Ladle the molten wax into the mould. Leave the wax to cool. A dip will form in the centre of the candle surface. Top up with more molten wax and leave to cool completely.

7 Carefully remove the candle from the plastic lid by pulling away the mould seal. Using a craft knife, cut through the tape down the side of the mould.

8 Remove the tape and finally peel off the cardboard from around the candle. Trim the wick.

RIGHT: Embossed candles in a variety of shapes and sizes add interest to any table setting. If you use a good proportion of beeswax to make your candles, the sweet natural scent will fill the room.

SEASHELL CANDLES

Using shells as candle holders is an excellent way to remind yourself of holidays by the seaside.
Shells come in a variety of shapes and sizes and they add greatly to the pleasure of setting a scene.
Collect a variety on your next holiday to use in this way.

YOU WILL NEED
- *150g (5oz) paraffin wax*
- *50g (2oz) natural beeswax*
- *double boiler*
- *metal-core wick for small candles*
- *shells in various sizes, well cleaned and dried*
- *sand-filled bowl or plate*
- *greaseproof (waxed) paper*

1 Melt the waxes in the double boiler and remove from the heat. Prime the wicks by soaking 15cm (6in) lengths of wick in the wax for 5 minutes. Place the shells in the sand-filled bowl or plate and bed them down firmly. This will ensure that they do not tip over when filled with wax.

2 Allow the wicks to cool on a sheet of greaseproof (waxed) paper. If the wax has begun to set, return it to the double boiler and melt once again. Carefully pour the wax into the shells. Do not overfill or the wax will drip out of the shells when the candles are lit.

3 Leave until the wax has partially set (small shells will set rapidly; larger ones will take proportionally longer). Push the primed wicks into the soft wax. The wick should protrude about 1cm (½in) above the wax.

OPPOSITE: The mysterious glow of candlelight is accentuated by the delicate shell holders.

HINTS AND TIPS
Use a variety of shells in different shapes and sizes to make unusual candles for dramatic effect. The metal-core wick used will burn a candle of up to 5cm (2in) diameter, so, if the surface area is greater than this on the larger shells, add one or more extra wicks: this allows for even burning and looks very attractive.

Whether you are looking for contemplative solitude or setting the scene for a romantic interlude, a candlelit bathroom will fulfil your requirements. The gentle glow of flickering flames combines with warm water to soothe away cares/troubles, impart a golden hue to the skin and make you feel calm and relaxed.

Take your candlelit experience a stage further by scenting the candles with essential oils, or add a drop of oil to the pool of melted wax at the base of the wick, once the candles are lit. This allows you to change the fragrance at will. Try rose geranium to lift your mood; jasmine for love, or bergamot to ease stress.

FLOATING CANDLES

Candles floating in a bowl of water are especially attractive. As the water moves gently, so the flames flicker and alter focus to create the most romantic atmosphere for that special dinner occasion. Specially coloured candles can complement your decor.

YOU WILL NEED
- *stearin (10% of quantity of wax)*
- *double boiler*
- *wax dye*
- *spoon or stirrer*
- *paraffin wax*
- *wax thermometer*
- *metal petit four moulds*
- *old baking pan*
- *weights (optional)*
- *primed floating-candle wick*
- *scissors*

MOULDS FOR FLOATING CANDLES

Metal petit four tins make ideal moulds for making floating candles, and come in attractive fluted shapes which give the candles a scalloped, flowery appearance. Any tin can be used so long as it has a smooth surface and is wider at the top than at the base, so that the candle will slip out easily when it has set. Look out for other interesting moulds which will produce patterned and embossed details on the candle surface.

1 Melt the stearin in the top of the double boiler and add the dye, stirring until thoroughly blended, then add the paraffin wax. Heat until the wax has melted and reaches a temperature of 82°C (180°F). Pour it carefully into the moulds and gently tap the sides to release any bubbles.

2 Sit the tins in shallow water in an old baking pan to help them cool, weighing them down if necessary to stop them floating about.

3 When the wax has started to set, a little well will form in the centre of each candle. Reheat the wax as before and carefully top up each candle until the well is full.

4 Push a length of wick into the centre of each candle while the wax is still soft but firm enough to hold the wick upright.

5 Leave until completely set, by which time the wax will have shrunk away from the sides of the moulds and the candles can be turned out. Trim the wicks to 1–2cm (½–¾ in) and leave the candles for several hours before burning.

RIGHT: Tiny shaped candles in vivid colours have the irresistible appeal of a candy store. Group the candles together in a glass bowl or float individual candles in shallow goblets.

DECORATING CANDLES

ONCE YOU HAVE MASTERED THE BASIC TECHNIQUES
OF CANDLEMAKING, THE POSSIBILITIES FOR CREATING
DECORATIVE CANDLES ARE ENDLESS. YOU CAN EITHER
MAKE CANDLES IN INTERESTING SHAPES, COLOURS
AND PATTERNS, OR YOU CAN DECORATE THE SURFACE
OF BOUGHT CANDLES IN A NUMBER OF WAYS.
WHATEVER METHOD YOU CHOOSE, YOU CAN CREATE
BEAUTIFUL CANDLES OF YOUR OWN THAT WILL ADD
SPARKLE TO ANY OCCASION.

TOP: *Decorate the sides of a candle with pressed flowers for a
delicate and pretty effect.*

LEFT: *Globe- and droplet-shaped candles are embellished with
foil bands and shapes and sequins for a quick decoration.*

41

STENCILLED CANDLES

For that special occasion, decorate your plain candles with stencils. These are easy to make and give added lift to your decor. Check that the stencil is tight against the candle. Round candles can be quite tricky to spray evenly so start with straight-sided ones until you become more proficient.

YOU WILL NEED
- *candles*
- *tape measure*
- *stencil card (posterboard)*
- *pencil*
- *ruler*
- *scalpel or craft knife*
- *spray adhesive or masking tape*
- *non-toxic spray paints*
- *lace or paper shelf edging*

HOW TO STENCIL

Cut out the design using stencil card (posterboard) or thin plastic sheet, available at craft suppliers. Alternatively, use bands of lace oddments, or paper doilies, to create delicate filigree designs. Use metallic spray paints: they add a glamorous shimmer and can be mixed together in light layers. Practise spraying the paint first on to waste paper and follow the manufacturer's instructions. Spray in short, controlled bursts and don't struggle to achieve a perfectly even finish: a slightly uneven texture is almost preferable.

1 To make a stencil to cover the whole candle, first measure its height and circumference. Then draw your design on the card cut to fit. Cut out the parts of the design that will form the pattern on the candle.

2 Fix the stencil firmly around the candle. Coat the back of the stencil with a light layer of a spray adhesive that allows for repositioning and stick it to the candle. Alternatively, put a length of masking tape where the two ends meet.

OPPOSITE: A diamond design, simple star and fleur-de-lys motifs and a lace effect will soon transform classically elegant, ivory church candles.

3 When the stencil is held tightly in place around the candle, apply the paint. Leave it to dry and then remove the stencil.

ABOVE: An equally effective method for a filigree effect is to cut lengths of lace to fit around the candle. Fix the lace in place with masking tape and then spray on the paint. Leave to dry before removing the "stencil".

GOLD-LEAF CANDLES

Gold leaf is unique and expensive. However it can be used to decorate candles to great effect and will add dazzling richness to a display. It is easy to apply once you get the hang of it. You can buy books of gold leaf in all good craft shops.

YOU WILL NEED
- *tracing paper*
- *fibre-tipped pen*
- *sheets of gold leaf transfer*
- *candle*
- *masking tape*
- *scissors*
- *ball-point pen or blunt-ended instrument*

TRANSFERRING DESIGNS

The easiest way to transfer the gold leaf design on to the candle is to trace a pattern on to the gold leaf transfer with a ball-point pen. To vary the thickness of the gold lines, you could try using a knitting needle or other blunt-ended instrument. Do not use anything with a sharp point. Always take care to apply even pressure and press only where the pattern is to be transferred. The negative pattern left on the used gold leaf transfer sheets can be used to decorate another candle. In this instance, you need to draw directly on the gold leaf transfer so that you can see exactly where the gold remains.

1 Draw your design on to tracing paper (the sheets from between the gold leaf transfers are ideal for this purpose because they match the gold leaf exactly in size).

2 Position a sheet of gold leaf transfer, gold side against the candle, and fix it firmly in place with strips of masking tape. Place the tracing paper with your design over the gold leaf. Fix it lightly in place with masking tape so that you can easily lift it off and reposition it later.

OPPOSITE: A touch of gold always makes any object seem more lavish – and using gold leaf is a simple way to bring a sparkle to pale candles.

3 Draw over the pattern carefully with a ball-point pen.

4 Peel back the gold leaf transfer, checking that all the pattern has been successfully transferred. If necessary, replace it and trace any parts again. Using fresh sheets of gold leaf transfer, and re-using your tracing paper design, repeat the above until a pattern has been applied all over.

MARBLED CANDLES

Mimic the natural mottling of marble with waxed dyed in two colours. You can choose dark colours
or pale shades to create marble, and stone effects using cream with muted yellow and red ochres.
See how effective this dramatic mixing can be.

YOU WILL NEED
- *dip and carve wax*
  - *sharp knife*
  - *double boiler*
    - *wax dye*
  - *spoon or stirrer*
  - *2 old baking pans*
  - *4 large sheets greaseproof*
    (waxed) paper
    - *rolling pin*
  - *paper template*
    - *primed wick*

ROLLING THE WAX

To make a paper template, draw a rectangle on paper 28 x 15cm (11 x 6in). On one of the two shorter sides, mark two points 17mm (just under $^3/_4$in) from the corners. Draw a freehand line from these points to the corners at the other end, curving the lines slightly. Cut along these lines. For a template this size, you need 270g (9½oz) of wax.

For a straight-sided candle with a flat top and base, trim the edges of the rolled wax into a rectangle before you roll it round the wick.

1 Cut half of the wax into chunks and melt it in the top of the boiler. Stir in the dye. Line a baking pan with greaseproof (waxed) paper so that it overlaps the sides, and pour the wax into the pan.

2 Melt the remaining wax and dye it in a contrasting colour. Prepare the second baking pan and pour in the contrasting batch of wax.

3 Leave the wax to set slightly and then place each wax in turn between layers of greaseproof paper and roll into a sausage shape. Knead the two contrasting rolls together. The two colours should be mingled but not mixed into a single colour.

4 Keeping the wax warm, put it on a clean sheet of greaseproof paper, on a flat surface. Cover it with another sheet of paper and roll out the wax until it is about 5mm ($^1/_4$in) thick.

5 Remove the top piece of greaseproof paper. Place the paper template directly on the wax and quickly cut round the edge with a sharp knife.

6 Press a length of wick along the widest end of the wax so that 2cm (¾in) extends above the top edge. Then roll the wax tightly and carefully around the wick.

7 Continue to roll up the wax, keeping it as straight as possible. Press the edge of the wax into the candle. Trim the base and the wick. Leave the candle to set for at least 1 hour before burning.

HINTS AND TIPS

If you are a newcomer to making candles, practise by mixing small quantities of different coloured wax on a sheet of greaseproof paper first before embarking on a large candle. Keep any leftover pieces of wax for re-use later.

RIGHT: *Marbled candles form excellent focal points in your decor.*

SCENTED CANDLES

Scented candles fill a room with a delicious fragrance as they burn. Add just a small amount of scented oil or wax perfume to the molten wax to create a romantic atmosphere. Aromatherapy oils possess therapeutic powers that can alter mental and emotional states, soothe and even heal.

YOU WILL NEED
- *card (thin cardboard)*
- *bowl*
- *pencil*
- *rubber mould*
- *scissors*
- *primed wick*
- *mould seal*
- *wicking needle*
- *paraffin wax*
- *double boiler*
- *wax dye*
- *spoon or stirrer*
- *wax thermometer*
- *wax perfume or scented oil*
- *needle*

HINTS AND TIPS

You can use oils produced especially for candlemaking or add essential oils, to give your candles individual qualities. Only add a small amount of scented oil to the molten wax when making perfumed candles; blend nine or ten drops of oil to every kilo (2 lb) of wax. Use a mould made of rubber or glass because the oil can damage plastic moulds.

1 Make sure the card (cardboard) is big enough to cover the top of the bowl. Draw around the mould on to the card, then cut out the outline. Push the mould into the hole.

2 Thread a primed wick through the mould. Make the burning end watertight with mould seal. Pull the wick taut and tie the opposite end of the wick around a wicking needle.

3 Melt the paraffin wax in the double boiler. Add the dye, and stir the two together. When the wax reaches 75°C (167°F) turn off the heat. Add the perfume or scented oil, stirring it into the wax.

4 Pour the wax into the prepared mould. Fill it just as far as the rim of the mould.

5 Fill the bowl with cold water and leave the candle to cool for 1 hour. Prick the surface of the dip round the wick with a needle, then add more hot wax to fill. Leave to cool for another hour.

6 When the wax is set and cold to the touch, remove the wicking needle and card. Gently peel back the rubber mould. Trim the wick back at the base and, if necessary, neaten the bottom of the candle by standing it in a warm saucepan to level off the surface.

ABOVE: Scent your candle with an appropriate perfume This one is perfumed with rose oil which creates a calming effect. The rubber mould used has an ornate Byzantine feel. Rubber moulds are available in more intricate designs than the plastic varieties and include flowers, fruits and vegetables.

PRESSED-FLOWER CANDLES

Nothing is more magical on a summer's evening than eating by candlelight. On still evenings, you can place candles in glass jars and eat in the garden. For a special event the candles can be decorated with pressed flowers and used as part of the table setting.

HOT WATER METHOD
YOU WILL NEED
- *deep narrow saucepan*
- *church candle, preferably one of the shorter and fatter shapes*
- *pressed rose heads*
- *a selection of small silver metal shapes, such as stars, flat beads or buttons*
- *tweezers*

2 Repeat the process, turning the candle each time and not leaving it in the water for too long, in case the wax melts around the decorated parts of the candle. A pair of tweezers will help you to push the heavier items into the wax.

MELTED WAX METHOD
YOU WILL NEED
- *white wax candles*
- *dish towel*
- *metal spoon*
- *cup of boiling water*
- *pressed flowers and leaves*
- *transparent glue*
- *cheese grater*
- *double boiler*
- *metal kitchen tongs*

1 Place each candle on a folded dish towel. Heat the metal spoon in the cup of boiling water and rub the spoon over the candle to soften.

1 Fill the saucepan with boiling water. Holding one end of the candle, dip the other end in the water for 4–5 seconds. Remove the candle from the water and immediately stick on as many of the pressed rose heads and decorations as you can before the wax hardens.

HINTS AND TIPS
Another method of fixing dried flowers to a candle is to use a heated spoon to soften the wax. You then need to dip the candle into hot wax to seal the flowers in place when the decoration is finished. Small, light objects are easy to fix, but heavier objects take more practice as speed is crucial if the decoration is to stick before the wax hardens.

2 Press a leaf in place with the back of the spoon. Fix all the leaves and the flowers on in the same way. Continue until the design is finished.

3 Coarsely grate another candle and melt the wax in the double boiler. Using the tongs, hold the decorated candle by the wick and dip it in the molten wax for a few seconds.

4 Smooth over the surface of the leaves and flowers with your fingertips while the wax is still soft. Leave it to cool and then repeat, holding the other end of the candle.

ABOVE: Church candles are the best for decorating with pressed flowers, as they burn for longer.
LEFT: Flowers and leaves create a delicate picture, and the decorated candles can be surrounded by flower heads picked from the garden, to give a natural country look.

SHAKER CANDLES

Candles can be decorated with simple shapes to reflect the style of the house and mood of the occasion. Here, simple shapes drawn from the Shaker tradition of North America, make a typical, attractive decoration that captures the essence of Thanksgiving.

- *sponge about 2cm (³/₄in) thick*
- *fibre-tipped pen*
- *scalpel or craft knife*
- *old baking pan*
- *greaseproof (waxed) paper*
- *paraffin wax*
- *double boiler*
- *deep red wax dye*
- *spoon or stirrer*
- *heart-shaped biscuit (cookie) cutter*
- *plate*
- *aquamarine water-based paint*
- *washing-up liquid (detergent)*
- *candle*
- *fine paintbrush*
- *wax glue*

HINTS AND TIPS
For a simple home-spun feel, candles can be decorated with sponged patterns and motifs cut out of wax. Biscuit (cookie) cutters come in numerous different shapes, from heart, star and leaf designs to gingerbread figures and farmyard animals, so the choice of motifs is wide ranging.

1 To prepare the sponge for the border design, draw four small squares, so that together they make one larger square which looks as though it has been quartered. Cut out half the depth of the sponge on two diagonally opposite squares.

2 Line the baking pan with greaseproof (waxed) paper. Melt a small quantity of wax in the top of the double boiler and add the dye. Stir until well blended.

3 Pour the molten wax into the lined baking pan. Tip the pan to spread out the wax evenly so that it forms a fine layer. Use the cutter to stamp out as many hearts as you need.

4 Mix the paint on a plate with a little washing-up liquid (detergent). Dip the sponge into the paint and press it on to the candle to make a border. Leave to dry.

5 Press a heart against the candle so that it becomes curved. Paint one side of the heart with wax glue and then press it firmly to the candle. Add more hearts at equal intervals.

HOLDERS AND CONTAINERS

The variety of candlesticks and holders available is huge, ranging from antique Georgian silver to plain wooden holders. Part of the fun of decorating with candles is adapting various objects into stunning candle holders, then using your imagination to embellish your home and enhance the magic of candle flames.

Top: Use your imagination to turn everyday objects such as cheese graters into dramatic candle holders. Here, they enhance a selection of candles set into silver and tin boxes.

Left: A variety of candle holders both simple, and ornate. Choose your accessories to suit your theme and your pocket.

INSTANT CANDLEHOLDERS

Many items can be pressed into use as candle holders. Among the most familiar are old wine bottles — simple and effective — but there are other items from the home and the garden that can be adapted into original candleholders.

ABOVE: *This lovely display of candles in delicate pieces of china is perfect for an elegant tea party.*

ABOVE: *Pieces of crystal and cut glass ornaments are worth hoarding so that you can make an impressive candle display for the right occasion. With a collection like this, you will have a shimmering, glistening atmosphere to chase away the shadows.*

LEFT: *Use large glass jars for taller candles. Make sure the tops of the candles reach close to the tops of the jars so the flames have enough oxygen. Half fill the jars with sand for stability and a seaside feel. Perfect for outdoors.*

ABOVE: *Halved coconut shells make impromptu holders for little candles. If you have time, paint the insides gold.*

LEFT: *Inexpensive embossed tumblers come alive when night-lights are lit inside each one. Here, a glass plate beneath the glasses adds to the sparkle.*

LEFT: *A simple collection of bottles filled with candles looks splendid on a windowsill. Here, a number of old bottles are complemented by Victorian glass decanters in different shapes and sizes. The candles used have been drawn from a range of colours that helps to draw the group together.*

ORGANIC HOLDERS

Autumn fruits and vegetables can be used to make dramatic seasonal candle holders. Here, gourds are embellished with coloured candles to complement the fruit. Wrap the candles with autumn-tinted leaves for added colour, but be sure only to use thick church candles for this.

ABOVE: Candles can be bought in the shape of fruits. Arrange them in a bowl for a merry effect, but keep a careful eye on them as they burn.

LEFT: Small green-striped squashes look charming holding apple-green candle stubs. They are quick and easy to prepare – simply hollow out the centre with an apple corer, then insert the candle. Tie on some autumn leaves with raffia, to finish.

RIGHT: Cut holes in a selection of gourds and fit them with complementary-coloured candles.

PUNCHED TIN HOLDERS

Simple patterns punched into tin cans help to make very pretty candle holders. To prevent the can from denting when the patterns are punched you need to fill it with wax. When you have completed your design, melt the wax to remove it from the can.

YOU WILL NEED
- *tin cans*
- *can opener*
- *tape measure*
- *tracing paper*
- *pencil*
- *scissors*
- *stearin (10% of quantity of wax)*
- *paraffin wax*
- *double boiler*
- *wooden spoon*
- *wax thermometer*
- *masking tape*
- *punch*
- *hammer*
- *bucket*
- *night lights or small candles*

PREPARATION
Soak the labels off the empty cans in hot, soapy water. Wash the cans carefully and let them dry. Smooth any sharp edges. Measure the height and circumference of the cans and then cut out a rectangle of tracing paper to fit these measurements.

1 For each design, fold the tracing paper in half and draw a pattern on one half. Turn over and trace the second half of the pattern. Unfold the paper and redraw any faint lines.

2 Measure the correct amount of cold paraffin wax. Melt the stearin and wax in a double boiler. When the wax reaches 82°C (180°F) pour it into the cans and leave to set.

3 When the wax is hard, fix the template in position with masking tape. Using a punch and hammer, gently but firmly punch out the pattern on the can.

4 When the entire pattern has been punched out, remove the tracing paper. Invert each can in a bucket and pour over boiling water to remove the wax.

5 Rinse the insides of the can with boiling water to remove any traces of wax. Remove the other end of the can with the can opener. Place the can over a night-light or a small candle on a plate.

ABOVE: Patterns punched into a tin can create an air of mystery and concealment where the light appears to arrive by magic from within. Be careful how you handle the cans as they can become hot to hold.

PAINTED CANDLESTICKS

New wooden candlesticks can be aged and mellowed using simple paint techniques to give an instant patina of age. The effect is intensified if the surface is rubbed back to the wood in places, with any extra knocks and chips further enhancing the distressed look.

FOR ANTIQUE-FINISH CANDLESTICKS
YOU WILL NEED
- *wooden candlesticks*
- *wax candle*
- *off-white emulsion (latex) paint*
- *small, flat and fine paintbrushes*
- *fine sandpaper or wire (steel) wool*
- *antiquing patina*
- *acrylic paints (smoke blue and jade green)*
- *varnishing brush*
- *matt (flat) varnish*

1 Rub the candlestick with a candle, applying a light coating of wax to any pointed edges and areas which would be most likely to have been damaged through wear and tear.

HINTS AND TIPS
Previously painted candlesticks are perfect to work with. There is no need to remove the old paint completely, just make sure that the surface is clean, dry and oil-free before you start. Sand the surface lightly with fine sandpaper to remove any varnish.

2 Paint the candlestick with off-white emulsion (latex) paint and leave to dry. If the wood shows through the paint, apply a second coat and leave it to dry thoroughly.

3 Lightly rub over the painted candlestick, using fine sandpaper or wire (steel) wool, to give a scuffed surface. Take the paint right back to the original wood in a few places.

4 Apply a coat of antiquing patina with a brush. Lift off some of the patina with a rag to mellow the painted surface and add texture.

5 Using a fine paintbrush, roughly paint bands of smoke blue around the top and bottom of the candlestick as well as inside any grooves. Leave the painted candlestick to dry.

6 Roughly paint thin lines of jade green within the smoke blue bands. Leave to dry thoroughly, then brush on a coat of matt (flat) varnish.

OPPOSITE: A craquelure finish and simple antiquing paint techniques can be used to make new candlesticks look suitably aged and antique. The effects of ageing are easy to mimic – with patience, paint and varnish you can create years of dirt and grime, knocks and scuffs in just a few minutes.

FOR GOLD CANDLESTICKS

YOU WILL NEED

- *candlestick*
- *gold paint*
- *paintbrushes*
- *craquelure (crackle) base varnish*
- *craquelure (crackle) varnish*
- *antiquing wax*
- *soft cotton cloth*
- *matt (flat) varnish*
- *varnishing brush*

1 Paint the candlestick gold, taking care not to let the paint build up in any grooves. Spread the paint with even brushstrokes. Leave to dry.

2 Brush on a coat of craquelure (crackle) base varnish. Brush it out smoothly so that no drips form.

3 Let the varnish dry naturally – this should take about 15–20 minutes. Then apply an even coat of craquelure varnish, making sure that the base coat of varnish is covered.

4 When dry, colourless cracks will have formed over the surface of the candlestick. Take a cotton rag and rub antiquing wax into the cracks. Wipe away all excess wax or pigment and then seal the surface with a coat of matt (flat) varnish.

INDEX

Advent ring, 17
autumn, 15

bathrooms, 9, 36
beeswax, 20, 28
    candles, 8, 11, 12
    sheets, 30
birthdays, 17

candle holders, 55–63
candlesticks, 10, 11, 12, 56, 62–3
Candy Twist Candles, 32
chandeliers, 9, 10
Christmas, 16–17
church candles, 11, 17
colouring candles, 24–5, 32
containers, 55–63
cooling, 26
country style, 12

dip and carve wax, 20
dipping can, 22
Dipping Candles, 24–5
double boiler, 22

Embossed Candles, 34–5
essential oils, 36, 48

Floating Candles, 21, 38
flowers, 8, 11, 14–15, 16, 50–1
foliage, 15

garden flares, 14
Gold-leaf Candles, 44
Gothic style, 10
gourds, 59

Hallowe'en, 17

Instant Candle Holders, 56–7

kitchens, 9

lanterns, 9, 12, 14
lavender, 12–13

Marbled Candles, 46–7
metallic spray paints, 42
mould seal, 21, 26
Moulding Candles, 26–8
moulds, 20, 22, 28, 34, 38, 48, 49

Organic Holders, 58–9

Painted Candlesticks, 62–3
paraffin wax, 20
Pressed-flower Candles, 50–1
Provençal style, 12–13

pumpkin lanterns, 17
Punched Tin Holders, 60–1

Rolled Candles, 30
rolling wax, 46

scent, 20, 36
Scented Candles, 48–9
Seashell Candles, 36
Shaker Candles, 52
silicone oil spray, 34
spiral candles, 32
sponging, 52
spring, 14
squashes, 58
stearin, 8, 20, 28
Stencilled Candles, 42
summer, 14

table settings, 8, 9, 11
tallow, 8
tapers, 8, 24–5
themes, 10–11
thermometer, 22

wall sconces, 9
wax, 20
    dye, 2
    glue, 20
weddings, 16
wicking needles, 23
wicks, 21
winter, 15